THE NOISY
AiRPLANE RiDE

By Mike Downs
Illustrations by David Gordon

TRICYCLE PRESS
Berkeley

STOMP, STOMP, TROMP

Down the Jetway with a grin,

take your seat and buckle in.

A vent above sends cool air.

It makes you blink and blows your hair.

CHUG, CHUG

The tug's hooked up;
 you won't be late.
Time to push back
 from the gate.

RRR-RRR-RRR

The engines start, one by one.
Smoke might puff when this is done.

WHiRRRR

On the wings the flaps slide down.

They'll help the plane get off the ground.

The wheels bump on taxi out.

Ground controllers choose your route.

Throttles forward, engines roar.

Down the runway, time to soar.

CLUNK

Wheels up

WHiRR

Flaps up

RATTA-RATTLE-SHAKE

There's bumpy air as you ascend.

See how the wings are made to bend?

THRUM, THRUM, THRUM

The engines hum throughout the flight,
never stopping, day or night.

The seat belt sign goes out. Flight attendants walk about.

Oh, no! You tipped your cup. That's okay, just wipe it up.

**The lavatory latch can slide
to make the sign show "occupied."**

KER-OOSH

Don't let the airplane toilet flush
scare you with its noisy gush.

CLiCK

Just push the button for some light,
and you can read this book at night.

DING

The sign's back on.
It's time to land.
You'll get to hear more
      noise again.

Thrum-ummmm

Throttles back, as you descend,
your in-flight cruise is at an end.

WHiRR

Flaps down

KERCHUNK-CLUNK

Wheels down

ERT-ERT

The wheels touch; you're on the ground.

Next, the pilots slow you down.

ROAR! ROAR!!

Reversers help the plane to slow
by changing where the thrust will go.

SHUDDA-SHUDDA-RRNNN

The airplane rumbles, sometimes shakes.

Lots of planes have noisy brakes.

WHiRR

Flaps up

THUMPiTY, THUMP

The wheels bump along again
as the airplane taxis in.

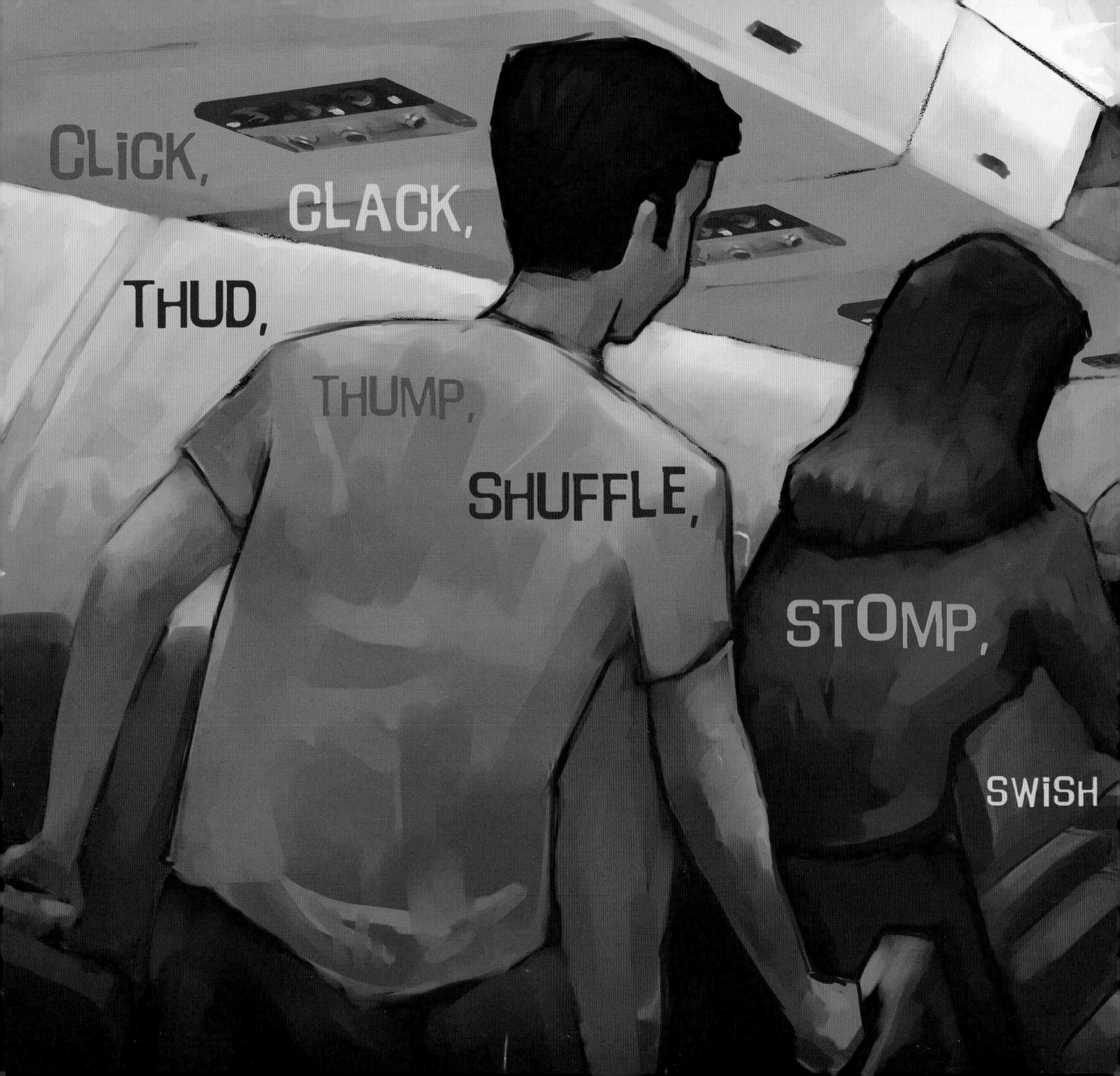
CLiCK,
CLACK,
THUD,
THUMP,
SHUFFLE,
STOMP,
SWiSH

At the gate you're almost done.
People take their bags and run.

HELLO!
OVER HERE!!

Hey, that sound's not from our ride.
It's Grandma waiting just inside.

OTHER THINGS YOU MIGHT SEE, HEAR, AND FEEL

POP!

EAR PRESSURE

Your ears may "pop" when the air pressure changes as the airplane climbs and descends. If it becomes uncomfortable, try chewing gum, eating, or swallowing to help ease the pressure.

QUEASINESS

Sometimes, especially if you're not feeling well to begin with, you may get an upset stomach when flying. Check the seat pocket in front of you and get out the bag. That way, if you need to throw up, you'll have it ready. No big deal.

AUXILIARY POWER UNIT (APU)

The APU sounds like a jet engine. Why? Because it IS one! The APU provides electricity and air-conditioning to the aircraft until the main engines are running, but cannot provide power to move the plane. Normally located under the tail, it is completely enclosed in the aircraft.

LUGGAGE

Yes, you CAN hear luggage. Listen for thuds and crashes underneath your seat during the boarding process. This is your luggage being carefully placed onboard.

VORTICES

If the air humidity is high (muggy weather), you might notice what appears to be smoke coming off the wing. Don't worry. It's fog, not smoke. This fog forms when the air pressure drops enough to cause water vapor to become visible. Spinning trails of fog near the wingtips are formed by the vortices (spinning airflow) at the end of the wings.

LEANING FORWARD AFTER LANDING

When the aircraft touches down, pilots use wheel brakes and thrust reversers to slow the airplane. This rapid deceleration (slowing down) may cause you to lean forward in your seat. In most cases, the pilots stop the airplane as quickly as possible in order to make a convenient turnoff, not because the runway is short.

MUZAK

Twing, twang, la, la, la. If you have impeccable taste in music, you might want to bring earplugs for this special treat during the boarding process.

ENGINES SURGING

The RRR-rrr-RRR-rrr sound of engines surging is common during the approach to landing phase of flight. Since the air is normally bumpier at lower altitudes (especially under puffy clouds), the pilots must constantly change the power setting in order to hold a precise speed.

SPEED BRAKES/SPOILERS

These panels raise up from the top center of the wing. In the air, they're used to descend more quickly. They're used during landing to help the airplane settle on the ground, which makes the brakes more effective.

FLAPS AND SLATS

Flaps, which are located on the trailing (rear) edge of the wing, and slats, located on the leading (front) edge, slide out so the airplane can fly safely at slower speeds—typically during takeoff and landing. You can see them deployed just after engine start and about ten to thirty miles from the airport before landing.

THRUST REVERSERS

There are different types of reversers. Some have a cowling (covering) that slides back, making it look like the engine has split in half. Some have panels that open in the middle of the engine. Others extend behind the engine. Reversers slow the plane by directing thrust from the engines forward. They can even be used to back up the plane.

FOR JOSEPH, MY EXUBERANT
PLAYMATE, COMPANION, AND SON – M. D.

FOR TWO AWESOME PILOTS,
SHIRLEY AND LAURIE – D. G.

Text copyright © 2003 by Mike Downs
Illustrations copyright © 2003 by David Gordon

All rights reserved.
Published in the United States by Tricycle Press, an imprint of Random House Children's
Books, a division of Random House, Inc., New York.
www.randomhouse.com/kids

Tricycle Press and the Tricycle Press colophon are registered trademarks of Random
House, Inc.

Library of Congress Cataloging-in-Publication Data

Downs, Mike.
The noisy airplane ride / by Mike Downs ; illustrations by David Gordon.
        p.   cm.
Summary: Rhyming text describes the many sounds associated with an airplane flight
and what they mean. Includes a section with more facts about airplanes.
1. Airplanes—Juvenile literature. 2. Air travel—Juvenile literature. [1. Airplanes.
2. Sound.] I. Gordon, David, ill. II. Title.
TL547 .D69 2003
387.7—dc21
                    2002011016

ISBN 978-1-58246-091-8 hardcover
ISBN 978-1-58246-157-1 paperback

Printed in China

Typeset in Imperfect and Will Robinson
The illustrations in this book were rendered using Painter 6.0 and Photoshop 5.5.

First printing, 2003
First paperback printing, 2005

9 10 — 16 15 14 13

First Edition

Random House Children's Books supports the First Amendment and celebrates the right to read